EARMAGEDDON

Silencing the Earbenders

LACRESHA HAYES

Arkansas Texas Louisiana

Copyright © 2015 Lacresha Hayes

All rights reserved.

ISBN: 978-0-9862057-9-8

All scripture quotations are taken from the King James Version of the Holy Bible, Public Domain.

Cover Design © 2015 Jesse Kimmel-Freeman

Publisher is Lanico Media House, an imprint of Lanico Enterprise.

Printed in the United States of America

Other Books by Author

The Rape of Innocence: Taking Captivity Captive

Becoming: My Personal Memoirs

Raw Redemption

Truth and Intimacy: A Couple's Journal

Poetic Infinity: Passion and Promise

Unnecessary Roughness

A Heart in Motion

Heart Strings

Cascade of Tears

The Ultimate Survival Guide for the Entrepreneurial Woman

The Path to Oneness

Adjacent Smiles

Tangled

Black Dakota

The Snare of a Strange Woman

Let Him Kiss Me

For the amazing relationships that never got off the ground, RIL!

ACKNOWLEDGMENTS i

INTRODUCTION 1

A GLORIOUS DISASTER: *A Note Of Consideration For Readers* 3

CHAPTER 1: *The Thirsty Ear* 6

CHAPTER 2: *The Earbenders* 8

CHAPTER 3: *Everybody Has One* 10

CHAPTER 4: *Gossip Gang* 13

CHAPTER 5: *Beware The Investigator* 16

CHAPTER 6: *At The End Of Chaos* 18

CHAPTER 7: *Mental Renovations* 21

CHAPTER 8: *Embracing the Blank Slate* 23

CHAPTER 9: *The Decision* 25

EPILOGUE 28

ABOUT THE AUTHOR 31

ACKNOWLEDGMENTS

There are a lot of people I could name in this book, appreciating the inspiration and information they brought into my life that helped me write on this topic.

Armetria Misha, who keeps the bar high and always happens to call when I'm being lazy. She keeps a fire burning under my gift.

Charles F. Stanley, whose books I've been reading lately and whose show has been instrumental in my spiritual growth.

Lastly, for my sisters on the net who I honor as strong praying ladies who are always ready with encouragement. I love you all!

EARMAGEDDON:

The final battle will rage on and on until the casualties mount up, bodies on top of bodies, until we overcome this subtly strong, seemingly benign but terribly deadly enemy. Gossip is a killer, my friend. Our job is to abstain from it and withstand any attacks by living our own personal truth with integrity.

INTRODUCTION

Your eyes lock across the room, or profiles lock across social media, as the case may be. You want to know her. You want to be with him. You wrangle up the courage to make an introduction. As the odds go, you're half expecting to be shot down but to your surprise, you find the other party is as interested as you are. You talk, laugh, and begin developing an intimate connection. After a certain time, you start to hope for something greater, like forever love. Dare you believe you can have the fairy tale? But you find that small ember of hope somewhere inside.

It's all googly eyes, smiles, blushes, and daydreaming, that is until…

Suddenly out of nowhere, the ear gets involved with others. Your sister doesn't like how she talks. Your mother doesn't like how he carries himself. Your friends have an opinion about appearance, jobs, possessions, and education. Seems, in fact, that everyone has an opinion about the person you've grown to love.

Then, once you two have sorted through opinions and put that animal to rest, you are immediately assaulted by the ear-benders. You know the ones… they always have something to tell you. Oh, but don't tell anyone who told you. You know the drill. They say they don't want to start trouble, which is exactly what they start anyway. The laughable part is that before you met your mate, you'd never heard their name. Now, everyone with a story is finding you to tell you something. At first, you listen because you are genuinely interested in knowing your mate more intimately. Truth be told, you envy those who had witnessed this wonderful life from any earlier point than yourself. You want to *know* your mate more intimately, make up for lost time. Then, as the information escalates into a full character assault of your mate, you listen out of fear because you don't want to be the next "victim" of his or her problems. You reason that maybe you need to know all of this information. It will teach you who you're dealing with, right?

As your ears split interest between the opinions and the gossip, they become unable to clearly hear the voice of your mate. You remember your mate, right? That's the person only weeks or months ago you were googly-eyed about. Now, the voice you once trusted enough to begin an intimate relationship with sounds like a potential enemy. It sets off a war between the mind and heart. So to clarify, the mind aks questions that only bring about unnecessary and often useless information. Because if you're honest, everything this person says to you is now filtered through the left ear filled with opinion and the right ear filled with gossip. Your heart, on the other hand, is petrified and your emotions are out of whack. One moment, you want nothing more than to love your mate without fear. The next moment, you're back fighting with your mate about what you've heard, how you feel, and what you want. Your relationship has now officially been infiltrated, and if the door to others is not shut immediately, it will not last, even if you two stay together.

Relationship is the cornerstone of all human interaction. But to relate, you must hear one another. Therefore, the enemy of relationships seeks to divide and conquer through distraction. He has launched an all-out assault on the ears. It's an earmageddon and the relationship casualties are astronomical!

A GLORIOUS DISASTER: *A Note Of Consideration For Readers*

If we begin at the last bad ending, wasn't that thing just a glorious little disaster? The attraction went wrong. After it all, maybe you told yourself it wasn't meant to be. Maybe you tried to explain away how you felt when you first saw him or her. I'm sure your mind has replayed the whole relationship a dozen times or more. You remember times that make you now wish you'd done something else, said something else or remained silent altogether. Or maybe the pain of remembering makes you regret meeting that other person at all. But after all the thinking, reflecting and tears, it is truly over. Regardless of who was at fault, both of you are going to have to deal with the fact that you're no longer together.

There are things that go bad and then there are things that go horribly wrong. Relationships that end because of outside interference almost always go horribly wrong. I mean, suddenly two people who once cared deeply for one another are now at odds. Each party has a "side" that fuels the fire and fans the flames of anger, hostility, and distrust. Her friends are telling her every bad thing they've heard now. His friends are telling him every horror story they've heard. Everyone is suddenly an investigative reporter coming back with the news of some happening that further alienates the couple from one another. And eventually, all that weight of outer influence breaks the bond that once held the two people together. Then, fueled by fear, each party turns on the other in an effort to protect themselves. Now, this is where a lot of relationships end, which is terrible. But there is a fate worse than death in relationships. Some of them stay together but become enemies caged together fighting for survival, often against each other. Either way, it is a sad reality for too many couples but it doesn't have to be so. That is the purpose of this book, to expose the dangers of having a relationship with open ear gates to outsiders.

Now, when a relationship ends, it would be nice if it affected no one outside of the couple but that is NEVER the case. Children are affected. The parents and other family members are often affected. Jobs can be affected since usually work performance is less than par. Friends, though, often either suffer or celebrate the most, a statement I think each reader should marinate on.

There are friends who celebrate break-ups simply because the mate was perceived as a potential threat to the friendship. There are friends who celebrate because they genuinely believe that their friend is better off without the current mate. And then you have friends who suffer because they loved both parties and a split often makes them feel torn between the two people. Some suffer just because they love the friend who is going through heart break. The above statements represent only four possibilities as it pertains to the suffering of friends, but not all of them suffer. Some of them truly celebrate your misery because they are not friends, even some of the ones who believe themselves to truly be a friend. There are endless heart issues that often make your friends the most unreliable source of support when you are in a relationship.

I decided to write this book for several reasons, probably the first and most important being that I needed a way to express the pain I've endured through betrayals that cost me relationships that I actually had high hopes for. But also, the invaluable experience I've gained in going through and coaching others who are going through break-ups needs to be shared with the world. Because on both ends of the situation are people, people who need healing. Not every friend knows how to be a friend and stay silent. This book may teach them when to speak. Not every person in a relationship knows whose voice they should listen closest to. This book will definitely teach them the core principles of a relationship.

Now before we move forward from this point, I need to add a strong statement that I hope every reader remembers the entire way

EARMAGEDDON: *Silencing the Earbenders*

through the book.

First, I know how scary it is to meet, date and maybe even marry a stranger. You don't want to be played, manipulated or hurt in any way. So, you think launching an investigation is going to protect you somehow. But the premise of this book is the exact opposite. The very foundation of this book is trust. TRUST. However, the first trust I'm asking readers to have is in the Creator. The second trust is in your own inner knowing that leads you to what is supposed to be in your life for whatever reason and however many seasons. Often, too much listening only seeks to drown out our own inner voice that is most true to who we are and what we need. It boils down to who you want to allow to be responsible for you: the outside world or yourself.

Second, we all have stories of times when the rumors maybe saved us from making a dating mistake, or even a friendship mistake. But I'm calling your memory to the stand right now. I'm asking you to remember how many times the rumors caused alarm that was unnecessary. I'm asking you to remember how many friends you almost missed because someone you know didn't care for them. I'm asking you to remember how many terrible things has been said or supposed about you. How often have people in the outside world been right about you? Now when you put those numbers together, you're going to discover that the rumor mill has cost you more than it has ever given. I'm sure if I presented this case in front of any jury, they'd find in my favor. Gossip and opinions are mostly wrong on some level and thus completely unreliable.

Based upon those two ideas, I'm calling my readers to embrace a new possibility and see the truest way to protect your heart, not by listening outwardly, but inwardly and upwardly. And so now, let's get into it.

CHAPTER 1: *The Thirsty Ear*

My grandmother used to tell me, "When you go looking for it, you'll find it." I hated that saying. I'm still not crazy about it because in an ideal world, there would be nothing to find. But we aren't living in an ideal world, are we?

I was in a Skype session with a particularly accomplished client one day. We were supposed to be discussing the details of her beginning another business. But two minutes into the conversation, the session turned personal. She was apparently at a loss to explain why she was constantly assaulted with gossip about her chosen man. She just couldn't seem to get her family and friends out of her business. At the time, I didn't know the next question would become the premise of this book, didn't even have plans to do this book. But I asked her a simple question. "Why are you still listening?"

Verbal communication often require two things: a party to speak and a party to listen. As life goes, we cannot control the actions of others, including whether or not they will say something we may or may not want to hear, as the case may be. The only thing we have dominion over is our lives, including what we do, what we say and what we believe.

This is a very noisy world. There is and always has been something to listen to. But it is our responsibility to decide what we will listen to. Right now, there are people clamoring for you to believe like them in some area that your heart is already fix, but because you've decided, their opinions and information don't move you. You hear what they say, but you're not listening. It never touches your heart and barely even registers in your mind. That's because when your mind is made up, the thirst of your ear in that area is sated. But when your mind is searching for answers, your ears and eyes become thirsty for information that can help the mind decide. This is not a bad thing. It is how we grow, in so many ways, and shows a certain unity in the functionality of our bodies.

The ear thirsts for information to feed the mind to help it make solid decisions. Often times when it comes to relationships, we find that information ready and waiting for us, but it is not always the right information. Not every source is credible, but the ears do not possess the ability to discern credible information. This too is left to the mind, sometimes with some input from the heart. But until whatever issue the mind is turning has been resolved, the ears will be on alert for any information that relates to the issue. And thirsty ears wielded in ignorance will always lead to ruin.

Don't get me wrong, it is also the thirst of the ears that lead us to great discoveries. Thirsty ears are always listening to learn more so that the mind becomes more aware. It's a most joyous gift that God has given us, making it so that no amount of learning can ever dull the desire to learn more. May education always be a choice drug!

However, there are times when our environment is not conducive to listening. There are some things we don't really need to hear. And when it comes to relationships, we must truly use wisdom about listening. Having thirsty ears to know about your mate is dangerous when you allow others to tell you more about them than they can tell you about themselves. I'm not indicting the matter of truthfulness of outside information. Rather, I am making a case for the blank slate each relationship should begin on, something we'll discuss later. Suffice it to say, your love is going to make you hungry for more of your mate, but that hunger was created to keep two people fully engaged with one another, discovering each other like a new secret every day. It was not created to seek out those who are all too happy to bend your ear with both true and false statements about your mate. Just because it's true doesn't mean it is relevant. And every lie is a cancer waiting to destroy you.

CHAPTER 2: *The Earbenders*

One day I was standing in line at a dollar store behind two ladies, friends I presume, who apparently both knew the checker in the next line. An argument ensued about what the two women had heard about the checker. The checker vehemently denied any knowledge of the rumor and said she'd said nothing bad about either of the other young ladies. They continued verbal assaults toward the checker and it slowed the progress of all lines down. The manager had to come over to intervene on behalf of her employee. The ladies were slinging names all over the place. Apparently, a lot of people had been talking to a lot of other people and it led to a hostile confrontation that inconvenienced everyone who happened to be shopping that day.

We've all probably seen times when gossip got out of control and it led to confrontations. In fact, almost every reality show is filled with confrontation and gossip. It's made to seem glamorous in Hollywood. Even when we witness the tears of the victims of gossip, we keep tuning in to hear more. It's an abusive cycle because gossip *is* abuse. Make no mistake about it. And the abusers in that situation are what I like to call earbenders. They always got some juicy tidbits to share, always have something to tell you later when you see them out and about, always seem to be sitting around a talking crowd, and always seem to be mentioned in the middle of some mess.

Now not all earbenders are infamous. You also have those who hide behind the veil of friendship and family. They've always been in your life, it seems. They are always "looking out" for you and keep you informed about anything wrong going on that you may not have ever known without them telling you. You know they love you. They have loaned you money, visited you in the hospital, took you shopping, out to eat, or even on a double date. You drive each other's cars and may even have keys to each other's houses. Still, that does not automatically qualify them to speak about your relationship. But they bend your ear anyway. They suppose that telling you what "they say" in the streets is going to give you a heads up or some kind of advantage. Maybe they even fancy themselves your protector and savior and refuse to let anyone into your life who isn't just right.

Regardless of what kind of earbender you happen up on, it yields the same fruit – mental confusion. Not all of them intend you harm, but intent doesn't count for much in the aftermath of rumors, which is almost always disaster.

CHAPTER 3: *Everybody Has One*

I remember shopping with a friend one day. She must have tried on three wedding dresses, which can be a lengthy process. Trust me on this. The excitement of seeing your friend in the first dress she tries on wears a tad thin by the third one. Of course, I had an opinion about each one of them. But do you know what I discovered in the process of dress shopping? I came to truly understand that my opinion in the lives of others doesn't count for much, but given at the wrong time, it can mean everything.

I liked the last dress most while she had secretly favored the first. When questioned about the dresses, I told her that the last dress made her look smaller and curvier. At hearing that, she chose the last dress. But it was clear to all of us that she was unhappy about the choice. We talked about it further while browsing bridesmaids' dresses. She had always dreamed of a Cinderella type wedding and the first dress had been her ideal dress. And so, I opined again and told her I think she should get her dream dress, even if it was out of her budget a little. Yeah, that's what friends often do, give bad advice. I had to chuckle as I wrote the last line, remembering how much I bonded with my friend during her special time, and all the times I shared a useless opinion and bad advice to make her happy.

Opinions are not endangered or rare. In fact, they are as common as a speck of dirt. Everyone has an opinion about something. All you have to do is bring a topic into awareness and you will be inundated with opinions in no time flat. And nothing gets earbenders talking faster than relationships. Everyone has an opinion about someone else's relationship. But not everyone's opinion should matter. In fact, there are only two important opinions in any relationship and they both belong to the parties who entered into relationship with each other. The friends of, family of, or even foes of either party need not even add their opinion to the number.

In a relationship, focus is extremely important. Ideally, the couple engage in conversations that increase in intimacy as their trust level goes up and as their bond is strengthened. Outside influence during the bonding period can do critical damage. I'm sure if relationships had autopsies, a great many, well over half perhaps, would be listed as a homicide and the cause of death would be outside influence. That's when people are carelessly giving opinions about who is dating who, or when people begin to volunteer information that isn't needed, much of which is unverified. Either way, the relationships die. The couples suffer. And way too often, the next people to enter into relationships with the displaced members end up suffering too. It is behavior that has to be cut off or out, like a cancerous mass. It will kill and destroy.

Part of the beauty of building a relationship is learning. Sure, you want your parents and siblings to like your mate. You want your friends to like him. You want your co-workers to like her. Nevertheless, the only person who *has* to like your mate is **you**. Only you will live with this person for the rest of your life. Only you know how you feel when you're with your mate, what good things this person brings out of you. Only you will have to be there for the good, bad, and everything in between.

At times, we go in search of someone else's opinion simply because we do not trust our own. We may even be lazy and don't want to invest the time in getting the information that will help us make informed decisions about our relationships. And then, there are times when we simply go in search of confirmation. We want to hear someone else say what we're feeling and thinking. Let's just be honest, especially for the women reading this book: there isn't any feeling greater than falling in love and having girlfriends to ooh and ahh with you, friends who like the person you like and don't know a bad thing about your mate. Even guys enjoy talking about their ladies with the guys, especially if she happens to be as beautiful outside as she is inside. People like to celebrate with other people. However, when you open the door to your relationships, when you put it on the table, assaults will come eventually. It's just the way of the world. You have to have some boundaries in place, both within and without. So celebrate, but set the boundary of how much input others can have on your relationship.

CHAPTER 4: *Gossip Gang*

Who hasn't been the subject of gossip? We have all heard something about ourselves that we were apparently unaware of until we heard about it. The grapevine is always jumping. There is always something to hear. Someone is always talking. Some people do it because they don't realize they are doing it since they've been doing it so long. Some people do it because it was done to them. Others truly believe it is harmless and they rattle off any information they have without much provocation. Yes, the gossip gang is ever employed, and well "paid" when we allow what they say to knock us off our square.

There was a particularly difficult time in my life after a break up that I was subjected to vicious rumors and gossip. I cried every day for weeks behind it all. I was getting mean messages on my social media, threatening phone calls, text messages, and I could not get away from it all. People were calling my probation officer with lies to get me revoked and locked up. Some of my things that were left behind were burned and some thrown in the ditch. With all the harassment I endured, a person would have thought the break up was my fault. But because my ex tried to commit suicide, everyone who loved him and everyone who loved drama descended on me like vultures. As horrible as it was to live through it, that scenario taught me an extremely valuable lesson about gossip and mobs. They run together. In fact, you cannot keep a mob or gang together without attaching it to the grapevine, even if the majority of what is said there is unreliable or completely untrue.

When you embark upon a relationship with someone, often it is a decision you make on your own, even in the case of hook ups. Ultimately, it is your decision whether you will deal with the person presented to you or not. Now in the beginning, asking questions is acceptable and expected. How else will you learn what you need to know about each other? The issue of this chapter is not asking questions and I want to make that clear. The issue of this chapter is who you question. Where and how you get your information is just as important as the information itself. Don't believe me? Look at your local courtrooms. People can be caught red-handed and get off the charges via technicalities. If they aren't informed of their rights and give a statement of guilt, it will not count in a court of law. The prosecutor cannot present hearsay as evidence either. There are all sorts of rules to govern the discovery of information to protect the individual who is charged and the integrity of the justice system. Why? Because not all information is reliable and even the truth can be used deceptively.

Your relationship is an entity and it has only three slots: one for you, one for your mate, and the last for God. When you add extra slots, you add confusion and dilute the bond between you and your mate. For every person you add into your relationship, you half your chances of being successful in that relationship.

I remember dating one guy who had quite the reputation. I didn't originally go looking for information, but it found me just the same. As I began to listen, I found myself caught up with the gossip gang. Before long, I had a new set of "friends" who always had something new to tell me about him. Because not all of it was bad, I'd sit and listen. I listened to people tell me about his last relationships, his money habits, his temper, his talents, and everything else. Even though I didn't want to admit it, the rumors were changing my attitude toward him. I loved him, adored everything about how he treated me, but the rumors had made me more watchful, paranoid, and even a bit bitter. I guess it goes without saying, we didn't make it. I could only hone in on one voice and I hadn't chosen his. I thought I was choosing him because I was with him every day, but I had chosen the voice of strangers to teach me about the man I had agreed to marry. Big mistake! Huge! Astronomical! You get the gist.

Gossip is infectious! It corrupts from the moment it enters the

EARMAGEDDON: *Silencing the Earbenders*

unguarded ear and it spreads quickly, silently, clothed under the guise of concern and self-preservation. When you sit down under the tutelage of the streets trying to learn about the character of your mate, you will get much more than information. You will also get, for all your trouble, a huge dose of fear and doubt.

CHAPTER 5: *Beware The Investigator*

As relationships develop, surface answers no longer satisfy. There are times when you're ready for information that your mate may not be ready to give. You may have questions he or she is unwilling to answer. And of course, there are times when we simply do not believe what we are hearing. In those cases, a lot of people want to discuss these feelings and this hunger for knowledge with others, be it friends or family. But here's what can happen when that door is opened.

After you make your relationship the topic in a manner that invites opinion or other outside input, people without restraint will pounce. They will take what limited knowledge they have and form opinions based upon their own experiences and then feed them to you. And if you make them feel somehow important or accepted during these intimate conversations, they will find themselves seeking more along the lines of your relationship, partly to impress you with knowledge once more, and partly because for the moment that they are involved in your life, they are not forced to deal with their own. Now please, allow me this rabbit hole because I'm taking you somewhere.

I was once a worry wart. Everything troubled me. I thought by worrying, I was loving. Now, I didn't accept this truth that came to me during my moments of meditation immediately. I had to sit with it for a while. Truth is, worrying about others often distracted me from worrying about myself. After all, their problems seemed easier to solve, from the outside looking in, right?

It is painful to sit with personal doubt and fear, knowing you're going to have to change something to overcome them. Self-awareness can be extremely difficult and requires discipline and courage. Rather than muster those and build a life they are enthusiastic about, it is much easier for people to find distractions. Discussing others takes the light off personal problems. Sometimes, it helps them feel better about the issues they are dealing with. For others, they actually care about you. And since they have nothing better to do, they'll appoint themselves your watcher or protector. But it all takes away from time that could be better spent repairing self. Nevertheless, busybodies are born every minute.

Busybodies are often investigators. Oh, you won't get them to admit it, but they are. They sit around various crowds listening, maybe even asking questions as your name and your mate's name comes up. They can sit in a circle that despises you. They can listen to people belittle you and your mate. After they sit around those dead, empty conversations, they come running back to you with the morsels of gossip. That's what you see. But if you could peel back the layer to the spiritual world, what has happened is this person is injecting poison into your veins, poison that can cause extreme heart dis-ease.

The investigator is especially dangerous to relationships, primarily because they tend to only report the worst information. They can hear four items of information, two positive and two negative. But when they report the news, somehow the good isn't mentioned or definitely is reported with bias that has a minimizing effect to the good.

Investigators are always burrowing. They visit your mate's page more than you do. They read every picture comment and follow any interesting "leads" gathered while searching your mate's social media. They are the ones who notice how often your mate likes your pictures, comments or posts your pictures. Isn't it funny how often they find themselves in a setting to hear some negative information? That's because they search for ways to know, but they aren't seeking to know the truth. They want to know that their opinion of this person is real. They are seeking collaborating evidence for their theory. Beware the investigator!

CHAPTER 6: *At The End Of Chaos*

At the end of everyone's opinion about your mate, and the rumors that circulate, at the end of all the worry and questioning, at the end of all the heart-rattling fear is a conclusion to the chaos. Pandemonium, like everything else, ends. Eventually, even the hottest fire will begin to dull in intensity. And gossip is a fire that cools, but in its wake leaves death. Isn't that always the end of chaos though? Death? But it doesn't always have to be the best of the relationship that dies, though many times it is.

There comes a time for those in a relationship that has been invaded by outside influence to make a solid decision. You see, the chaos comes in through minds that are not made up about one another. Once invaded, the only way through it is to actually make a solid decision. It comes down to actually facing the bedlam and deciding to either continue or discontinue the relationship. And even more than that, a solid decision has to be made about whether outsiders will continue to have a space in the relationship if it continues.

During a phone session with a client a couple of years back, I asked my client about his wife's involvement in his future business. That opened the door and his story came pouring out. He told me about how he'd made mistakes in the early part of the marriage, and how painful it had been to realize how much he'd hurt his family. She'd left for a time, which brought him to his senses. He said he'd decided not to try to get her back until he knew for sure he was ready to truly treat her as she deserved to be treated.

He told me that they'd gotten back together and he'd made her promises he never intended to break again. But after years back together, he said he is still greeted with distrust, questions, doubt, and hostility behind it. He went so far as to say he was having problems wanting to stay in the marriage himself. He didn't feel he could continue on with the constant distrust.

Months after our conversation, he and she began Christian couples counseling. He later told me that the very first thing the counselor recommended was for them to take some time away from family and friends, and reconnect with each other. The counselor had quickly recognized that her friends and family were the ones who couldn't forget his past and they took every opportunity to remind her of it. A wound that is constantly assaulted will never heal. I'm glad that they made it and recently celebrated 13 years of marriage.

While the above couple chose each other and took steps to evict outsiders, there are many more who keep trying to start over without addressing the issue of interference. Eventually, either they are broken and stay together miserably, or they call it quits. The pressure simply becomes too much after a while.

It is plenty difficult enough to deal with personal insecurities as it relates to meeting the long term needs of a mate, and maintaining a mutual happiness. If there is the added burden of pleasing family and friends, it takes energy away from the primary relationship. And let's just be honest here. It is impossible for your mate to satisfy both you and all the people who love you.

At some point, both parties to a relationship are going to be required to come out strong on the side of the relationship or on the side of other interested parties. It may seem a small thing to ask a question because the mother and father are concerned, but that is the exact type of pressure that weakens the relationship bond. It may not seem like much to come home from church with a mouth full of what the preacher thinks and what your fellow members have said about how your relationship should progress. But the truth of the matter is, no one has the authority to define a relationship if they aren't in it.

For some people, the damage done by interference is irreparable and they lose out on each other. For some, repairs are made and the relationship bond is secured, if not strengthened. But the best route to a healthy relationship is to keep outsiders outside of it. When the best route has already passed you by, the next best thing is immediate eviction.

CHAPTER 7: *Mental Renovations*

You cannot ever bond and build a secure relationship as long as the noise of the outside world has place in it. If, after all the drama, you decide to stay in the relationship, you must learn how to eliminate interference.

It isn't at all easy to tell your parents and family, or closest friends to mind their own business. There are times when choosing your relationship actually means cutting some other people out of your life, or at the very least, distancing yourself from them.

If you've gone through quite a bit already, your mind is likely filled with clutter and useless information, open questions, major and minor concerns, etc. You have made your choice and chosen your mate, now you must literally de-clutter your mind and make the necessary renovations to repair the damage done to you in places others cannot see.

Your mind is powerful. In fact, scientist are still discovering the almost limitless potential of the human mind. When your mind has been infiltrated for a period of time, it is easy to lose track of what is true for you and what comes from programming from other people.

As a minister, coach, and consultant, I give out a lot of advice. However, when it comes to relationships, I am slow to speak. And when I do offer counsel, I try to focus on what the person in front of me can do to become stronger and better, to find comfort and gain clarity. Almost always, my first piece of advice is to have people divorce the opinions of their loved ones. It is so important to reconnect with your original design before it was polluted with fear and doubt. First, you have to rediscover yourself, and then rediscover your vision for the relationship.

In the beginning, you had a dream, goals for your relationship. You saw a picture of yourself with your mate, saw you both being happy together. You must erase everything that is contrary to that original picture. Take each rumor, each attack, and every opinion one by one and decide that they aren't important. Whatever has happened, has happened. There is still love. And where there is love, there is victory.

Prime the walls of your mind and paint it a fresh, bright, inspiring color full of your hopes and dreams unhampered by fear. Look at each rumor and every character-assaulting thing you've heard as a hole in the wall. Put some puddy in and screen it. Prime it and paint right over it. You are not obligated to remember your pain and disappointments. Don't allow pain to continue coloring your life. You can choose differently. You can do the work. You can overcome and become more than you once were.

CHAPTER 8: *Embracing the Blank Slate*

At the beginning of a new relationship, or at the point of making a solid decision to trust or forgive and remain, there comes a blank slate. The blank slate is a beautiful blessing.

I remember when lined pages were not as common as it is now. I often used printer paper for various reasons. The beautiful thing about printer paper is there are no guidelines attached to it. You can do anything you want to it. You can draw, write, doodle, or all three. Think of your new beginning in this way. There is nothing there to forgive because all has been forgiven. There are no lines of tenderness to avoid crossing. There is only the pencil with a fantastic eraser, and the paper. It's time now to create.

The first aspect of creation is to decide what you want to create. You already know now what you don't want. You don't want drama. You don't want a free-for-all. You don't want distrust, paranoia, discomfort, and constant fighting. You want love.

1 Corinthians 13 lays out the very definition of love and brings great clarity in what should be the standard in how we love others. It speaks of love's patience, kindness, and humility. Though the entire chapter deserves a serious read, let's start your blank slate here to overcome the fear of loving someone else:

Love never fails... 1 Corinthians 13:8

The first obstacle and really the final obstacle is fear. Fear of giving it all and coming up with nothing. Fear of falling in deep with someone who is not in deep with you. The Bible helps us by telling us love never fails. It will not fail because there is not failure in love. How can it fail when it only seeks to give? And giving is a choice you make that no one else can take from you. So on your blank slate, you can remember that as long as love is your guide and your path, you cannot fail at whatever you draw, write, or doodle.

Sometimes when you begin again, there is also the fear that letting go of the offenses of the past will make you susceptible to going through the same thing again. Whatever fear presents itself in your new beginning, 1 John 4:18 tells us:

There is no fear in love; but perfect love casteth out fear: because fear hath torment. He that feareth is not made perfect in love.

Embracing your new start means divorcing the pain and damage and offense of the past. Even if you decided to move on with someone new, you cannot leave your past unforgiven. You cannot carry the open wounds into something new, bleeding all over your new love. And even more than that, if you decide to start over with your current love, you must exercise discipline to leave the past out of the new. In both cases, let your new start be a truly new start.

Yes, your past held lessons. But once a lesson is learned, there is no reason to continue recalling it except to encourage or instruct others, as a testimony, if you will. Your past should never be used as a weapon against you. Likewise, you must decide to never use anyone else's past as a weapon against them. Easier said than done. But this is the principle that keeps hurts and disappointments and life-sucking bitterness of past wrongs out of today and the joys that now holds for us.

CHAPTER 9: *The Decision*

You already have seen it go wrong a number of times. You may be single right now because of gossip. Maybe you picked up this book because you feel as if you're suffocating in a sea of rumors. You're tired of trying to sort through it all. You're tired of fighting with the person you once adored above all. If so, then now is the time for you to make that solid decision we spoke about earlier.

In one candid session with a client, she confessed she felt as if her mate had broken her heart repeatedly. As we explored her feelings, she began to realize it was not actually him who'd broken her heart repeatedly. For all the months of confusing chatter she'd endured and the questions that never seemed to yield a satisfying answer, it was now dawning on her that it had not been so much his actions that caused her pain. It was imposed suppositions by others. And as that realization hit her, she was suddenly stricken with an epiphany. It had been her all along. It had been her choice to listen to others, to question her mate through suspicion rather than trust. She'd chosen them over him and that had been the beginning of her problems in the relationship.

For another client, after the grapevine brought her proof of infidelity with her husband, she went through a divorce. After a few years, she found herself going through the same thing again, although this time, the rumors had been largely exaggerated. She and her mate decided to work through the issue and she decided to bar everyone out of their intimate place. They are now happily married.

You see, at the end of whatever happened and whatever was supposed, a decision still must be made. It always comes down to what you choose. This book does not seek to encourage you to stay in or let go of any relationship. The decision of this chapter is if you will continue allowing your decisions to be manipulated by vicious rumors, gossip, opinions, suppositions, and fear.

If I were indicting gossip, opinions, and unnecessary information, I could produce millions upon millions of witnesses against them. The tears of wives who walked out on innocent husbands. The tears of men who married the one the "people" chose rather than marrying the one they wanted. Tears of the old single lady who could never quite find herself satisfied because she lost sight of what she actually wanted as she borrowed opinions from friends and family. Tears of the man who lost the woman who truly loved him because they never learned to trust one another. I could bring in the children who watch Mom and Dad argue over the mysterious "they" who always has something to say. I could bring in the employers who have had to fire an endless number of people over workplace gossip that turned distracting and even hurtful. Oh, the list could grow so long that we'd never have time to present all the witnesses. Gossip has ruined more relationships and lives than anything else in the world.

So now, you come to this place where you have to decide to grow beyond the self-doubt that makes you susceptible to listening and reacting to gossip. Many people wait to feel some supernatural strength or unction to overcome this weakness. But deliverance from doubt and fear is first a choice.

In fact, most of your relationship is as simple as a choice. You must decide to be in it; decide the parameters of the relationship with your mate; decide to forgive (because no matter who you date, you'll eventually have to forgive something). Most especially, you'll have to decide to be happy in it. As it pertains to relationships, for a relationship to work, all it takes is for both parties to keep choosing their relationship daily. And to keep choosing to be happy in it. Sounds simple, feels complex, but ultimately, it is the truth.

During one session, a client and I discussed the power of choice. She told me she'd done all the right things in her marriage. She recounted all her love and sacrifices. Her husband had cheated and created a scandal for her. She didn't understand how her decisions could have affected the outcome of his. In fact, I talk to many couples who believe they are doing all they can and are disillusioned by a mate who has a more lackluster approach to the union.

Fact is, your choices are enforced in your life. You cannot decide for others. Even if somehow through the gossip and opinions, an ugly fact is discovered, and even if the mate you love is revealed to be anything but the person you thought you fell in love with, ultimately the ball is again in your court. Rather than focusing on the problem and getting lost in the emotions surrounding your situation, you need to decide what you will do. Will you forgive? Will you stay? Can you deal with the revelations? Are you mature enough to build beyond the damage? Are you strong enough to choose mercy, kindness, and love? Can you keep the infectious talk of the streets, and the obvious disapproval of family at bay and out of your relationship going forward? Can you do it for any new relationship you embark upon?

Until you can quieten the noise of the voices screaming in your head, you will forever be double-minded and a weak decision maker. Until you shut off the feelers to find validation outside of your relationship, until you tune the grapevine out, until you reclaim your ears and attention from the earbenders, you'll find yourself running on a wheel that goes nowhere, much like the hamster.

You don't need them. You don't need their knowledge. You don't need their validation or approval. You don't need their permission. God created you with everything you need and the answer of who to spend your life with is there as well. There is no lack in you, and from that place of wholeness, you can decide to trust the God in you again and finally be free of the turmoil that comes along with giving dominion over your life to others.

EPILOGUE

When I first started this book, I was determined to make the case for keeping others out of your relationships. I do understand there are times when a nosy neighbor or family member actually seems to save the day by bringing you information you would have never known otherwise. Maybe you had a situation in which you were in a relationship with someone who was not trustworthy and full of lies and deception. You credit your friends with saving you from heartache, but I beg to differ, and believe me, I've been there and done that too.

During a particularly trying relationship, I was convinced my boyfriend was doing things he shouldn't be. I heard the rumors and saw the texts and phone log. It got so bad that I found myself perplexed. And while I grew in distrust for him, I also grew in distrust for myself, which kept me running in circles. I'd turned into an investigator and was constantly invading his privacy and constantly finding something else to question or wonder about. His excuses always seemed believable to my confused mind. Because while I didn't trust him, I didn't trust myself to make a good decision concerning him. So I literally felt trapped in an unhealthy relationship, mainly made unhealthy by me, not him, even though he had cheated and lied. What?! Yes, he did wrong but it was within his rights. Follow me here.

The goal of a relationship is to grow together, building something as unique as the parties involved but bigger than both. It is **NOT** about molding or changing each other. It isn't about control. So, when a relationship begins, each party needs to put in the effort to learn who they are relating to. You cannot honestly form a bond through the eyes of others. So even if the person you desire has a questionable history, that too must be put in perspective by you according to what you want and need. Letting others in muddies the waters, and it will cause you to question yourself more than you question anyone else. Losing your ability to discern and your faith in your decision-making skills will hurt you way worse than discovering your mate does not deserve trust.

 Further, what one person cannot handle and color in the worst light may not even register for you if someone doesn't point it out. You wouldn't believe how many of your desires and fears are actually borrowed, because you listened to someone who had them and then after hearing their case, adopted them as suitable for you. Terribly sad!

 In my case, I wanted fidelity. I've always been taught that fidelity is the biggest thing. So, the thought of him being unfaithful made me paranoid and fearful. I began acting out of that fear and I violated the rules of relationship. Instead of accepting various facts about him and deciding how important they were as it pertained to the continuance of our relationship, I began whining, questioning, accusing, and nagging. That made me an unhealthy person to have a relationship with. It was not his actions that brought that out of me as much as it was the interference, the suggestions and suppositions of those close to me, the uncertainty of it all brought out the absolute worst in me. I'd given myself over to confusion. Finally though, a person gets tired of hurting, wondering, questioning and crying. So when I got tired, the first thing I felt led of the Spirit to do was invite others out of my intimate life. I divorced their ideas, fears, and even the information they brought me. I went back to the beginning and replayed the relationship for what it was to me. And then I decided, a decision I have yet to regret.

 When it comes to standing up against those you love on behalf of a relationship you cannot be sure will work, it can be extremely difficult. It may make you feel like you're falling to pieces because you want everyone to be happy. You don't want to hurt your mate, but you don't want to be separated from your family and friends. You don't want to not listen to them because what they think means so much. Lastly, you don't want them to think you have someone else more important than them in your life. You just want everyone to get along, love each other, and your life to be perfect. But here's what you have to see.

First thing is you cannot make anyone happy. Happiness is all personal choice, even in the midst of tragedies and definitely at all other times. You must learn to make yourself happy. Happy does not mean free of problems or disagreements. So if your mate is who you want to create a life with, then choose your mate. This is your life you're building and family and friends with any level of maturity simply have to understand that. You need no one's approval to be in a relationship with the person you love. It is a three way between you, the person you're with and your God.

Also remember, always remember, that no one else has to live with your decisions like you. Letting others be the reason you're either in or out of a relationship is the fastest way to misery and life-sapping disappointment. Stop hiding behind others because you're afraid of the consequences of your decisions. Truth is, you may make a few mistakes. Fact is, you'll make way more listening to gossip, opinions, and busybodies who bring back information you don't need anyway. A mistake you make while being true to yourself will teach you and make you stronger. A mistake you make listening to others only brings pain, confusion, and regret. And it is my hope, beloved, that you are tired of living with regrets and confusion.

HERE'S TO A HEALTHY, HAPPY, INTIMATE RELATIONSHIP!

ABOUT THE AUTHOR

Lacresha Nicole Hayes is the author of more than 30 titles, writing under two pen names.

Lacresha is the owner of Lanico Enterprise, publisher at Lanico Media House, an independent Executive Vice President with myEcon, Inc out of Georgia, a successful grant writer, and a prolific author.

Lacresha mentors new entrepreneurs, women and authors. She is the founder of Your Healing Partner, a women's holistic coaching program, and travels extensively to spread awareness about abuse, as well as to train and inspire people all over the country.

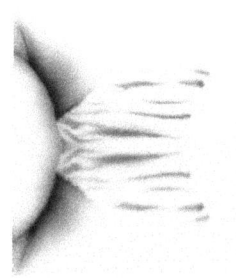

www.ingramcontent.com/pod-product-compliance
Lightning Source LLC
Chambersburg PA
CBHW061310040426
42444CB00010B/2572